W9-BHY-818

01/2019

A Note to Parents

THIS BOOK is part of an exciting four-level reading series for children, developing the habit of reading widely for both pleasure and information. The series is designed in conjunction with leading literacy experts, including Dr. Linda Gambrell, Distinguished Professor of Education at Clemson University. Dr. Gambrell has served as President of the National Reading Conference, the College Reading Association, and the International Reading Association.

Beautiful illustrations and superb full-color photographs combine with engaging, easy-to-read stories to offer a fresh approach to each subject in the series. Each DK Reader is guaranteed to capture a child's interest while developing his or her reading skills, general knowledge and love of reading.

The four levels of reading books are aimed at different reading abilities, enabling you to choose the books that are exactly right for your child:

Level 1: Learning to read
Level 2: Beginning to read
Level 3: Beginning to read alone
Level 4: Reading alone

The "normal" age at which a child begins to read can be anywhere from three to eight years old. Adult participation through the lower levels is very helpful for providing encouragement, discussing storylines, and sounding out unfamiliar words.

No matter which level you select, you can be sure that you are helping your child learn to read, then read to learn!

For Dorling Kindersley
Senior Editor Laura Gilbert
Jacket Design Mabel Chan
Managing Art Editor Ron Stobbart
Publishing Manager Catherine Saunders
Art Director Lisa Lanzarini
Associate Publisher Simon Beecroft
Category Publisher Alex Allan
Production Editor Sean Daly
Production Controller Rita Sinha
Reading Consultant Dr. Linda Gambrell

For Lucasfilm
Executive Editor Frank Parisi
Art Director Troy Alders
Story Group Leland Chee, Pablo Hidalgo,
Matt Martin, Rayne Roberts
Director of Publishing Carol Roeder

Designed and edited by Tall Tree Ltd
Designer Sandra Perry
Editor Jon Richards

First American Edition, 2016
Published in the United States by DK Publishing
345 Hudson Street, New York, New York 10014

Page design copyright © 2017 Dorling Kindersley
Limited
DK, a Division of Penguin Random House LLC
16 17 18 19 10 9 8 7 6 5 4 3 2
013–178076–Feb/2011

© & ™ 2017 LUCASFILM LTD

A catalog record for this book is available from the
Library of Congress.

ISBN 978-0-7566-8279-8 (Paperback)
ISBN 978-0-7566-8278-1 (Hardback)

DK books are available at special discounts when
purchased in bulk for sales promotions, premiums,
fund-raising, or educational use. For details, contact:
DK Publishing SpecialMarkets, 345 Hudson Street,
New York, New York 10014
SpecialSales@dk.com

Printed and bound in China

A WORLD OF IDEAS:
SEE ALL THERE IS TO KNOW

www.dk.com
www.starwars.com

Contents

STAR WARS™

THE CLONE WARS

DON'T WAKE THE ZILLO BEAST

Written by Jon Richards

Watch your step!
Some creatures are
friendly.
Other creatures are
dangerous.

Zillo (ZIL-LOH) Beast

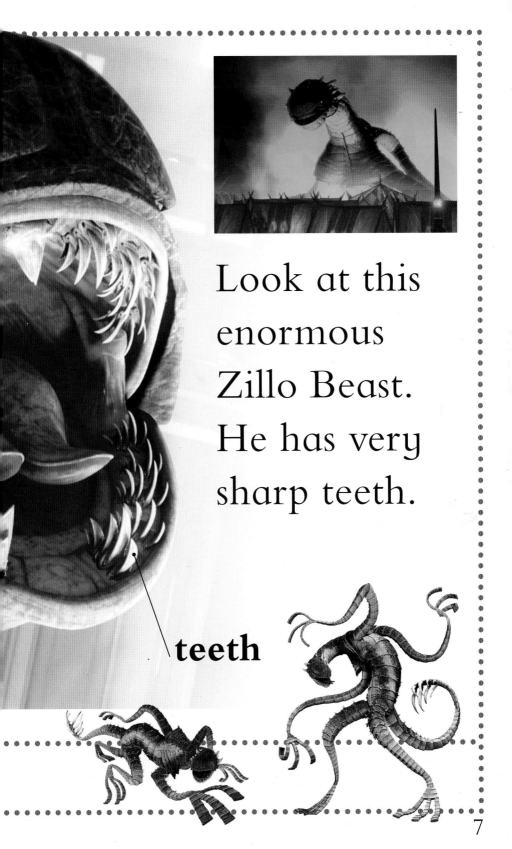

Look at this enormous Zillo Beast. He has very sharp teeth.

teeth

Look at these
hungry gutkurrs.

 gutkurrs (GUT-CURS)

spikes

They have spikes
on their backs.

Look at this kwazel maw.
It has colorful marks
on its body.

marks

kwazel maw (KWAY-ZELL MOR)

leg

11

Look at this
Rishi eel.

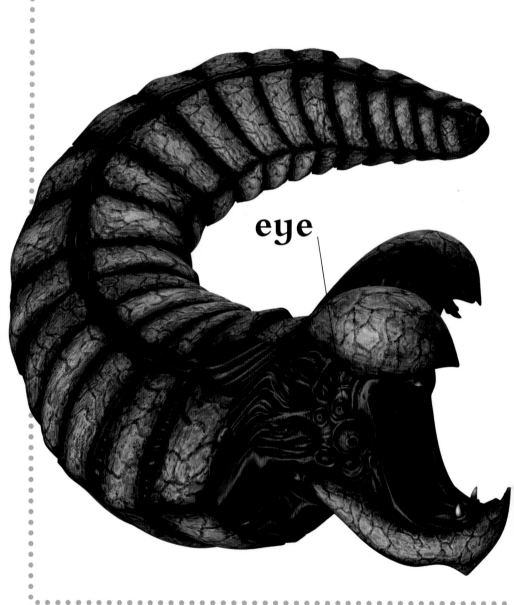

eye

Rishi (REE-SHEE) eel

It lives inside dark holes on a cold moon.

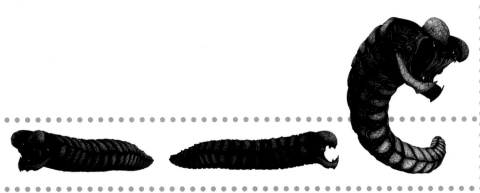

Look at this angry
gundark.
It has four very
strong arms.

**large
ears**

gundark (GUN-DARK)

arms

trooper

skalder (SKOLL-DER)

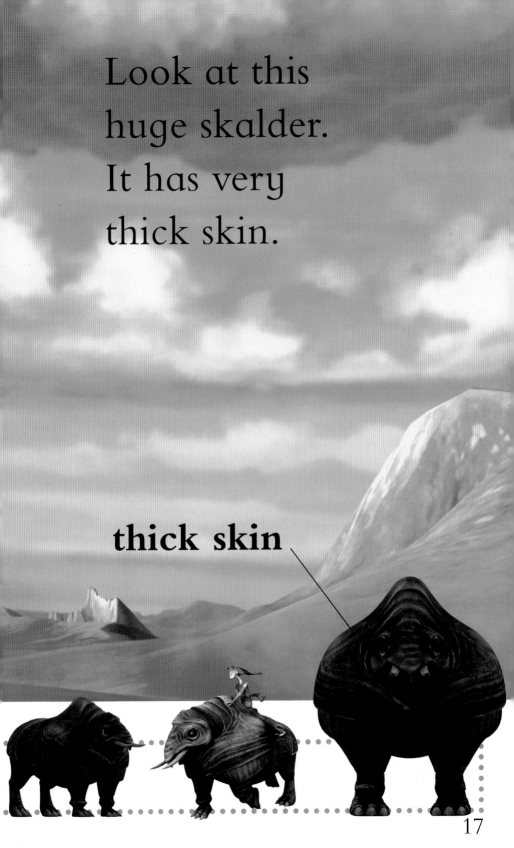

Look at this
huge skalder.
It has very
thick skin.

thick skin

Look at this mastiff phalone.

beak

mastiff phalone
(MASS-TIFF FAA-LOAN)

It has a sharp,
pointed beak.

ice

narglatch (NAR-GLATCH)

Look at this spiky
narglatch.
It lives on an icy moon.

rider

Look at these peaceful shaaks.

shaaks (SHOCKS)

They live in groups
called herds.

Look at this flying xandu. It flaps its powerful wings.

xandu (ZAN-DOO)

wings

Anakin
Skywalker

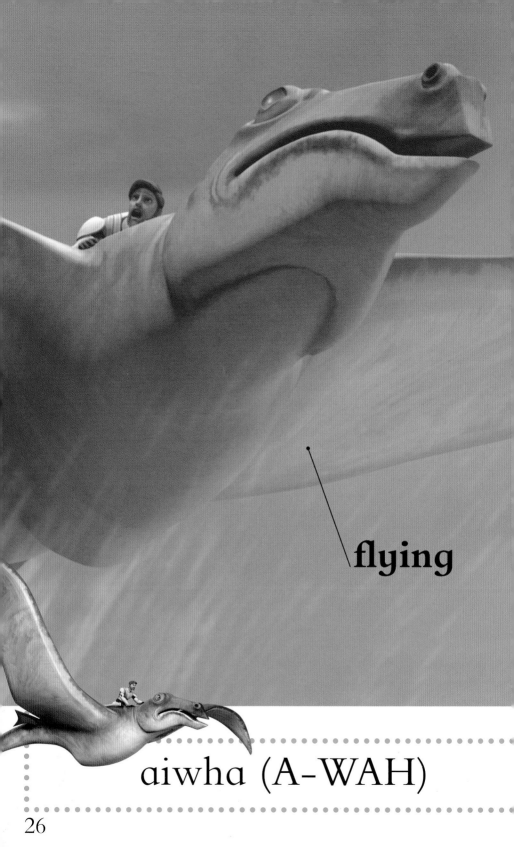

flying

aiwha (A-WAH)

Look at this massive aiwha. It can fly through the air.

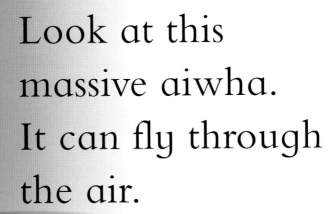

swimming

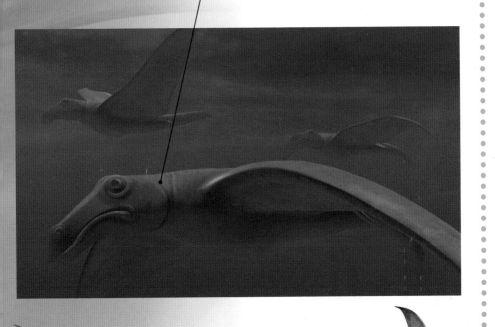

Look at this
scary roggwart.
It has sharp claws
and robot arms.

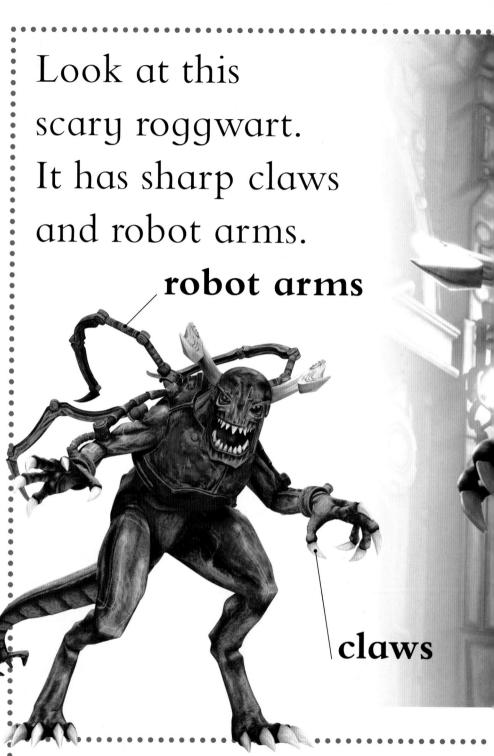

robot arms

claws

roggwart (ROG-WORT)

29

Now you have met the creatures.

Which is your favorite?

Glossary

Herds
large groups of animals

Marks
patterns on an animal's skin

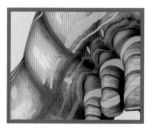

Moon
a small object that goes around a planet

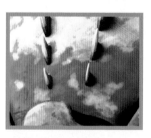

Spikes
pointed parts of the body

Teeth
parts of the body that are used to bite and chew food